LOOK WHAT I CAN SEE

A PRESCHOOL BOOK THAT TEACHES COLORS, SHAPES, NUMBERS, AND MUCH MORE!

To Lulu
from Granny
Christmas 2021

To Lucia

Joanne Sandlin

By Joanne Sandlin

Illustrated by Tracey Burner

ISBN-13: 978-1480276987
ISBN-10: 1480276987

NOTE TO PARENTS:

In addition to enjoyment, this book offers many educational concepts. These include Counting, colors, shapes and numeral recognition.

Other educational opportunities include beginning math concepts (counting), language development, nature awareness (seasons), rhyming words, and listening.

Building self-esteem and following directions are two valuable concepts for success as your child enters school. This book is designed to build a strong foundation of each.

Adults will enjoy the special bonding time with their child as they discover the joy of books and the fun of learning.

Joanne Sandlin

PARENTAL SUGGESTIONS:

You may ask your child additional questions beyond those directions given on each page to enhance their thinking skills. This will also build their inquisitiveness of the world around them which will increase their learning.

email: AuthorJoanneSandlin@gmail.com

DEDICATION

This book is dedicated to all of the wonderful children who have passed through Westside Recreation Preschool who have inspired this book, and for all the children who will learn from it in the future.

ACKNOWLEDGEMENTS

Thanks to my wonderful husband Russ for his support and encouragement while writing this book.

A special thank you to Tracey for capturing in her art the joy and fun of learning about the world.

JANUARY

Pointed trees and snowmen
Make a winter scene.
Name all the shapes
That you can see.
Find the colors
Red, white, black and green.

FEBRUARY

Pretty cards say, “I love you.”
Name the colors, then
Count the shapes.

Are there three
or two?

I
U

MARCH

Pointed kites are flying high.
Name the shapes
and the colors in the sky.

APRIL

Fluffy spring bunnies
With long oval ears,
Tails so soft and round.
Hidden in the grass so green.
Name the colors of eggs
To be found.
Can you count the oval eggs?

MAY

Bright spring flowers;
Colors everywhere.
There are flowers tall
And flowers small.
Can you see
That none are square?

JUNE

Get a pole
And set sail –
Find some oval fish
With a triangle tail.

The boat has a shape or two.
If you can name them,
Please do.

Are there any shapes
Hiding under the sea?

JULY

Fireworks popping
On a clear summer night.
Bursting with colors –
What a fun sight!
Name the colors,
Pretty and bright,
Then name the shapes
That light the night.

Name this shape of the moon.
Sometime it has another shape;
Tell what it is if you know it, too.

AUGUST

The seashore
Has a shape or two.
Find a round sand dollar
And a starfish.
Is the ocean blue?

A seagull watches
From a cloudy sky.
Can you find it
And say, "I spy."

SEPTEMBER

There's a cool nip
In the Autumn air.
What's your favorite,
Crunchy apples or juicy pears?
What color is your
Favorite fruit?

This season has another name.
Is that why the leaves
Do the same?

OCTOBER

Triangles, rectangles
And pumpkins round.
Shapes are everywhere
To be found!
Name some that you see.

FOR
SALE

NOVEMBER

November has a special date
Potatoes and pie
May fill our plate.
Big round turkeys
With many shapes.
Name the shapes and colors
That you see.

DECEMBER

December is a time
With wonders everywhere,
And bright colored presents
In rectangles and squares.
Stars and circles on a tree
Making people happy as can be.
Cookies round and candies square.
Name the shapes and colors you can see
All around the Christmas tree.

The seasons four
Fill our year
With sounds and smells
In the air.
Look all around you
Everyday.
Find colors and shapes
Everywhere.

Summer
Winter
Autumn
or Fall
Spring

Go back and find your favorite page.
Why is it the one you like best?
Think about all you have learned.
Look around your house
And outside in your town.
Every day tell someone you know
Something you have learned!

8
3
6
4
9
7
Name the numbers you can see.
1
10
5
2

The author, Joanne Sandlin, is a retired Founder/Director/Teacher of Westside Recreation and Parks Preschool, Taft, California, having earned an Early Childhood Education degree from Taft and Bakersfield Colleges. She also taught Developmentally Disabled adults at Westside Training Center in Taft, CA. She volunteered countless hours at Taft and Tehachapi libraries, telling stories to delighted children and writing a column, "The Library Corner," for the *Tehachapi News*.

In addition to writing recipe columns in two newspapers for 16 years and publishing a cookbook *The Front Burner* with family and friends, she has been published in magazines such as *Maitre D'*, *Country Decorating Ideas*, *Country Discoveries*, *Colorado Country Life*, *Dun Rovin'*, and *Country Woman*.

She contributed many devotionals to church newsletters. Recent publications were two anthologies by Hidden Brook Press (Canada) featuring recipes and the accompanying stories that made them family traditions.

She moved to Prescott, AZ with her husband in 2003 and has two adult children. Professional organizations include Professional Writers of Prescott and Northern Arizona Word Weavers. Her inner child still likes to come out and play and enjoy the beauty in the world each day!

The artist, Tracey Souza Burner, an art major, graduated Connecticut's Norwich Free Academy in 1991. Tracey lives in Pennsylvania with her husband and their three children. She has illustrated two children's books by Rosemary Reagan Hall (*The Kids Knee Garden* and *Knock Turtles*) and produced black and white drawings for an instructional book titled *High Achiever Piano Instructor* by Roger Hayden. In addition to artist/illustrator pursuits, Tracey home schools her children and teaches art classes.

Made in the USA
Las Vegas, NV
19 September 2021

30646382R00024